Endorsements

For a good, solid learning experience with a smattering of rich humor, I suggest you take hold of Mark DuPré's *How to Act Like a Grown-up*. You won't want to put it down until you are finished. I am still smiling.

— GAVIN MACLEOD
Actor, *The Love Boat* and *The Mary Tyler Moore Show*

Just before reading *How to Act Like a Grown-up* I had just finished reading an autobiography of Benjamin Franklin, a man who was known for his common-sense proverbs and his everyday wisdom. I feel that Mark's book delivers the same theme. Mark addresses everyday situations with an incredibly clear common-sense approach. It is refreshing, humorous, and practical. I believe that it will serve to help and encourage many of us to put on our "adult clothes" and stand up as adults. Thank you, Mark, for opening our eyes to the obvious. Compliance to these principles will make the world a better place to live.

—WILLIAM G. BAXTER, M.ED.
Director of Family Counseling and Mediation Services

This should be required reading for everyone over the age of sixteen. As a person who had very little help growing up, I found Mark's book to be full of information that I wish I knew twenty years ago. Even at the age of forty, I found knowledge that I can use today. As a mum of two young boys, I know what an uphill climb parents have these days. Parents will find many tips in steering their children in the right direction. Mark's no-nonsense manner shows how to carry oneself without resorting to condescension. The common sense advice offered is perfect for an age when common sense is not so common.

—Lynda O'Rourke
Mother of two

This is a deftly written book whose light touch and humorous tone make its serious message easy and quick to understand. Whether we're young or old, acting like an adult requires knowing and adhering to societal norms, which Mark reminds us are as necessary to individual success as to the success of our civil society. What our parents taught us about appropriate behavior was right, and Mark helps them out by refreshing and updating their advice and reminding all of us about the importance of the social contract and the Golden Rule. And Mark knows what he's talking about—as a wildly successful university professor for more than two decades, he knows how to deliver information in a way that is listened to and remembered.

—Dr. Tina Lent
Chair/Professor, Fine Arts Dept., College of Liberal Arts
Rochester Institute of Technology

THIS BOOK IS AWESOME! I read it from cover to cover in one sitting. Mark DuPré's observations in *How to Act Like a Grown-up* are invaluable. Mark examines everything from cell phone etiquette to being on time, from divesting to investing. As I read the book, there were moments when I thought, "Yes, get them—finally someone is addressing this!" But then there were those moments when I was challenged to act like a grown-up myself. This is an excellent resource, empowering us to swim upstream in an age of extended adolescence.

—Dr. H. Lee Joyner, Jr.
Lead/Teaching Pastor
Christ Church, Gaithersburg, MD

I smiled though this book because it contains very direct instructions from a man who has submersed himself into community—he has seen what works and what doesn't. Too many adults are figuring this stuff out in their thirties and forties because they didn't have folks in their lives who were straight-shooters with them on the how to's of social behavior. Teens and adults alike should read this book and use it as a discussion starter in a small group.

—HEATHER R. STEVENSON
Artistic Director, PUSH Physical Theatre

How to Act like a Grown-up is an enjoyable and easy read! It felt as though I was sitting across from my wise grandfather as he taught me the lessons of life. It has made me think twice about being late and helped me to realize how self-centered tardiness can be. This is the perfect book to give to anyone who is looking to gain some wisdom in their life!

—DANIELLE WINDUS
Danielle Windus Cook Properties, LLC

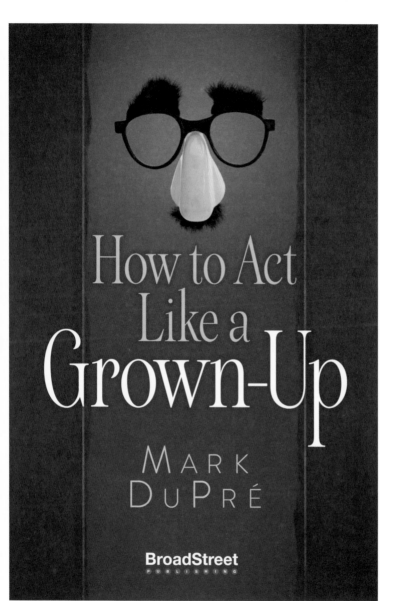

How to Act
Like a
Grown-Up

MARK
DUPRÉ

BroadStreet
PUBLISHING

BroadStreet Publishing Group, LLC
Racine, Wisconsin, USA
www.broadstreetpublishing.com

How to Act Like a Grown-Up
Witty Wisdom for the Road to Adulthood

ISBN-13: 978-1-4245-4988-7 (hardcover)
ISBN-13: 978-1-4245-5022-7 (e-book)

Cover design by Chris Garborg at www.garborgdesign.com
Typesetting by Katherine Lloyd at www.TheDESKonline.com

Stock or custom editions of BroadStreet Publishing titles may be purchased in bulk for educational, business, ministry, fundraising, or sales promotional use. For information, please e-mail info@broadstreetpublishing.com.

Printed in China

15 16 17 18 19 20   7 6 5 4 3 2 1

Dedication

To the woman who started me on my journey to acting like a grown-up and to the one who is working so hard to complete it.

To my mother, Mary Katherine Murphy DuPré, who treated me like a grown-up from my earliest days and showed me that sacrifice, love, and humor were worth striving for. And to my wife, Diane Roy DuPré, who really is a grown-up and keeps working patiently with me on getting there myself. Miss you, Mom. Love you, Diane.

Contents

"You have to do your own growing
no matter how tall your grandfather was."

Abraham Lincoln

"Children have one kind of silliness,
as you know, and grown-ups have another kind."

C. S. Lewis

Preface

Every generation complains about the one that comes after it. The complaints are pretty much the same: they're too loud, they don't show any respect, and their music is terrible. (If you're hearing this from older people now, don't worry. You'll have your chance with the generation that follows you.)

But if you listen closely, there are some truths to be learned between all the complaints. We all need to grow up, no matter what our age. There are some things that real grown-ups do and think that don't change over time, and life gets better if we learn what those are. There's nothing sadder than a person with a grown-up body and a mind and heart that haven't caught up yet.

In the hopes that you won't end up one of those, I offer these observations on how to act like a grown-up. Sometimes just looking at the right way to act or to think about something is a great way to begin to go from child to adult. Certainly a person can do all the outward grown-up things and still be a jerk inside—no book can prevent that. But I hope that laying out a few grown-up behaviors and perspectives will encourage you toward a quicker maturing process, which will benefit you and everyone around you. And life is just plain easier when you're an adult and acting like one.

Please note that I don't presume for a minute that most people over the age of twenty-one—myself included—actually do these things and think these thoughts all the time. The viewpoints contained here are just as challenging to me as they might be for you. I'm still working on growing up. (I didn't get a whole lot of help when I was younger.) I'd just like to share some of the hard-won observations and perspectives that have helped me along the way.

1

Be a Real Winner

~c◯:◯ɔ~

I f you're just heading into the adult world, or if you've been in it a short while, you've probably observed all the members of both teams playing in a competition getting trophies just for competing. Or you've been part of a class where every student has been told he or she is amazing and everyone's a winner, or where children learn to sing songs of praise to their own wonderfulness. If so, I'm sorry. You've grown up in a world gone crazy—in more ways than this book can address. One of the biggest challenges of people growing up now is the need to throw off the silliness about everyone being a winner and automatically being a remarkable and special human being.

In a competition,
someone wins and someone loses.
Or one team wins and the other loses.
That's life, and it doesn't affect
a person's worth one bit.

Technically, we're not all winners because we all can't win. In a competition, someone wins and someone loses. Or one team wins and the other loses. That's life, and it doesn't affect a person's worth one bit.

Let me set the record straight: we are all worthy of respect because we are human beings. We all have inborn dignity. We need to know that for ourselves—always—no matter what happens to us. We also need to remember this when we deal with others: everyone else is as worthy of respect as we are.

More than being worthy of respect, all individuals are special because they are the one and only *them* alive. It's a cliché, but it's true: only *you* can be the best *you* possible. You're here for a reason, even if you don't know yet what that is. No one has your particular combination of gifts and talents—no one! You may not be as good-looking (as society defines it) or sing as well or be as smart as someone else. But you have a family and a circle of friends and neighbors and a set of opportunities and talents (probably many of them still hidden at the moment) that make you a one-of-a-kind.

Once you've settled it forever in your heart and mind that you have value, please don't stop there! Don't camp out at a place where you're always insisting on your own worth (even just to yourself) and then doing nothing because you're worthy already. Build on that worth! Yes, you're special—so *do* something with it. Get better at what you can get better at, knowing that there will always be some who will do it better than you and some who never do it as well as you.

Don't let anyone or anything tell you you're not worthy of respect. And don't let anyone or anything—including yourself—stop you from building on it. What makes someone a winner is not that he or she is unique—everyone is! It's what we do with what we are and have that makes the difference. And that's what makes a person a winner.

2

Being on Time

Being on time used to be called *punctuality* (an old English word that used to mean something). It's also called being a decent human being. So be on time.

If you're consistently *not* on time, that's because you have developed your own personal system that gets you to places late. Something has to change in that system, and you're the only one who can change it. Here are some relevant thoughts:

- Your time is not more valuable than anyone else's, at least not all the time. So making people wait is not nice, and very selfish. If you make six people wait ten minutes for you, that's a whole

If you're consistently not on time, that's because you have developed your own personal system that gets you to places late. Something has to change in that system, and you're the only one who can change it.

hour of time you've stolen. We can't get back time in our lives, so don't take any from other people.

- You're probably doing one or two things that you should have done earlier, or things that could have waited until later. What are those things? Once you know, either do them earlier or do them later. So put on your big-boy or big-girl pants and resist the temptation to do that one more thing if you even *think* that might contribute to being late.

- Get your clothes ready the night before. And if that involves ironing, do *that* the night before too. (If you're not sure what ironing is, ask an older person—they might remember.) You'll be happy you did, even if you are generally not in a hurry in the mornings.

I heard someone say that if you're on time, you're late. So try aiming for early and see how it goes. What did you do to make that happen? Now do that a lot.

You're going to be wrong. Often.
That's not a problem.
Not admitting you've been wrong is.

3

Being Wrong

~CC!QƆ~

News flash: you're going to be wrong. Often. That's not a problem. Not admitting you've been wrong is. And not learning from being wrong is a big problem and can result in your becoming an official jerk. And no one wants that.

Acting like a grown-up means being able to admit that you've been wrong without a lot of drama and without kicking yourself either.

If you were wrong because you didn't know something or had some wrong information, that's usually not a big deal. Unless you invested your entire identity and course of action into something that you were wrong about, it shouldn't be too hard to tell yourself that you missed it. But here is what you have to do: take the new info and reevaluate everything around it. Change the information you *thought you knew* into the information you now *know*, and then hit a big subtotal button about the whole situation. You should come up with a new perspective that is different and better. (That's not just acting like a grown-up—that's *being* a grown-up.) It's going to be challenging to adopt the new point of view at first, but give it time to sink in.

If you were wrong about something and then *acted* on it, things get trickier because you've taken a situation and invested something in it. (See the chapter on Investing.) You have to divest (also in that chapter), and that's harder than just admitting you were mistaken. After you admit you were wrong, ask yourself what you need to do to clean up the mess.

When you misjudge how to grab something on the kitchen counter and it spills on the floor, you know what you have to clean up. It's all right there in front of you. When you've been wrong, you have to think long and hard about what might need cleaning up. Did you trash somebody wrongly? Swallow hard and tell the people you spoke to about it that you were wrong. Did you do something beyond talking? Do your best to reverse it. It will probably make things better. But even if it doesn't—or can't—it will make you a better person because you walked through the process of trying to make things right.

I once found myself in an incredibly difficult and awkward situation that involved many people. But only I and one other person really knew the whole situation, and it was important for many reasons that things not be blasted all over the place. Some former friends heard some wrong things, didn't ask for the correct information, made huge assumptions and judgments, and then sent me (and this other person) an explosive letter with a number of specific points that they were angry about. All their points were wrong because they were based on incorrect or incomplete information.

When the dust settled and I dealt with the fact that I'd lost a couple of friends, I realized how hard it was going to be for them to ever admit they were wrong because they acted so decisively based on inaccurate information. If they had only gotten the whole truth before writing, or hadn't made a wrong judgment based on bad information, it might not have been so hard to correct things. But they made such a huge investment in their wrongness, I'm not sure they will ever be able to admit that they were wrong about anything connected with what happened. That's sad.

Try never to get into that kind of situation. If you've been wrong, man up or woman up and admit it as quickly as you can. Reevaluate the situation or the person, and change your views. Then do what you hope someone would do if he or she were wrong about you.

It's no insult to find out you've been wrong. It stinks, but try to be happier that you learned the truth instead of bummed out that you were wrong.

4

Buying Stuff at a Store

~⌒⊂◯⁚◯⊃⌒~

The Golden Rule ("Do unto others ...") is easy when it comes to shopping.

If you're paying by check, make out the check while you're waiting in line (yes, and even sign it). Or even better, make it out ahead of time. No one likes waiting in a line while someone slowly and carefully fills out a check. (And some people get really annoyed when the culprit takes the time to do all the math in the checkbook, something he or she can easily do a few minutes later.)

If you don't know what a check is, not to worry. If you pay by cash or credit or debit, pull out your money or

You *will* be asked to
pay for the things you're buying,
so save everyone time and have
some form of payment ready.

card before the cashier gives you the total amount. Some folks act as if they never thought of reaching for their purse or wallet before the register person mentions it. Breaking news: you *will* be asked to pay for the things you're buying, so save everyone time and have some form of payment ready. And if you want to do the exact change thing, get your change ready in advance.

And really, fifteen items means fifteen items. It's annoying and rude when people sneak their twenty-plus items onto the fifteen-items-or-less conveyor belt. So don't do that.

What goes around comes around. So be the person you'd like to have ahead of you in line.

A ringing cell phone has some kind
of primal call to our psyches,
demanding to be picked up.
But you don't have to—really.
You're in control of that.

5

Cell Phones

~CO!OU~

Cell phones were originally thought to be communication devices and were used occasionally and only when communication was important—like when you had to be picked up, or when you were in trouble, or when you ran out of gas.

A cell phone has now become some sort of appendage—an extension of your personality instead of just a tool. And that makes it hard to use one like an adult, especially since the technology is still so new that lots of adult users are acting like children.

OK, we get it. The cell phone is part of you. But that just means you have to get a couple of things clear so you don't advertise how immature you are with one.

Don't talk loud. In the beginning, apparently a lot of people had to speak up to be heard. You would think that problem would be solved by now, but everyone I know has a loud-person story to tell. If you're having a hard time hearing the caller or being heard yourself, move somewhere else where you can raise your voice without being irritating, or turn up the volume on your phone. If you still can't hear the caller well, that's God's way of saying that you should talk another time. Tell him or her you'll call back.

Get it settled in your mind that the people you're actually with usually trump whoever is calling. There is no rule that says you have to take a call if you're speaking with someone. Learn the all-important nine-word question that shows your maturity: "Can I call you back in a few minutes?" Or better yet, let the call go and call the person back later. People understand emergencies, but real emergencies are few and far between.

Acknowledge the people you are talking to before speaking to your caller. Ask them if it's OK to take this short call, and then keep it really short. Or ask them to give you a minute and you'll try to keep it brief, and then keep it brief. If you really have to take an important call, excuse yourself from the conversation with apologies and say some version of "See you later." With all the communication options available, we have to pull together as grown-ups, or at least people trying to act like grown-ups, and respect the people we share physical space with.

And speaking of space, do your best not to answer the phone in crowded places like elevators, grocery store lines, or subways. Confined spaces seem to make cell phone conversations that much more annoying. I know that a ringing cell phone has some kind of primal call to our psyches, demanding to be picked up. But you don't have to—really. You're in control of that.

And last, if you happen to pick up a call when you're in the bathroom, don't tell the caller where you are. And please don't flush before you hang up.

Wild clothes work best with people who already know you, or when you are trying to make a statement that doesn't involve others getting to know you as a real person.

6

Clothes

~⌒◦⌒◦~

Unless you're in fashion or are a performance artist, you are not your clothes. Dress comfortably and appropriately, and only call attention to yourself if you're supposed to or if you don't want people to see the real you.

It's a fallacy to think that if people are so shallow as to judge you by your clothes, it's their problem. Well, what else can you expect if you dress strangely? Looking ridiculous is OK sometimes—I've done it myself when performing. But crazy clothes call so much attention to themselves that the people talking to you sometimes can't see the real *you* because your clothes are so distracting. Most people don't want their clothes doing the talking for them. Wild clothes work best with people who already know you, or when you are trying to make a statement that doesn't involve others getting to know you as a real person.

If you're going someplace special or different, try to keep the event in mind when you dress. Unless it's an "express yourself" party, remember what the event is and work with that. The classic "Don't ever wear white to a wedding" is legitimate because it distracts from the bride, and that's rude. Think about where you're going and make adjustments in your clothing accordingly. If the occasion is dressy, go for it. If it's casual, relax and dress that way. Be confident that you can handle any number of clothing styles.

I hate ties and am not completely convinced that they are not a diabolical scheme of some sort. But I've been to gatherings wearing everything from tuxes to bathing suits. I usually try to find out what the expected clothing style is. At one time, I did that because I thought I'd feel weird to be the odd man out. It's still partly that, but it's also that I want to make sure I honor the occasion—and the people involved—appropriately.

I am not my clothes. And most occasions are not about me anyway.

7

Comparison

⌐⌐⌐⌐⌐⌐

As long as there are people, there will be comparison. Other people and our own brains will always be making comparisons, consciously or not. Unfair comparisons can hurt, of course, and we need to be on guard about the damage they can do. But saying, "Don't compare," is pretty useless.

It reminds me of stress. When I was in the business world, I noticed a shift in training over the years. In the beginning, there were sessions on "stress reduction." Then apparently the folks doing that kind of training looked around and realized that was an unwinnable battle for most people. Then we had sessions on "stress management," which made a lot more sense to everyone.

Let's release the positive power
of comparison by changing our focus.
Let's stop deepening the rut of
comparison that leads to feeling
bad about ourselves.

Comparison is like that. We're never going to get rid of it, but we can manage it. In fact, we can even make it work for us. How? Well, by different thinking and changing our perspectives.

Most of us think of comparison as a bad thing, and we need to get away from thinking like that. Comparison can be a learning moment for all of us and a big help if we let it. For example, if we shift our thinking, we begin to realize how much we can learn by looking at others the right way. Over the years I've learned through comparing myself to others how to be gentler, how to handle difficult situations, and how to have healthier perspectives on any number of things. If we think of ourselves as lifelong learners and of everyone else as the source of life lessons, we can learn every day.

Of course the big thing to work out (notice I didn't say "avoid," because that's impossible) is resisting the kind of comparison that's accompanied by attacks on yourself. Noticing that someone is a better athlete than you, for instance, or is better looking, can offer you the choice of turning in on yourself and listening to voices that generalize and condemn: "See—you're no good at this sport," or, "I'm ugly." Let's learn to resist those voices! The fault here isn't comparison itself; it's listening to the negative voices that can accompany it.

Let's release the positive power of comparison by changing our focus. Let's stop deepening the rut of comparison that leads to feeling bad about ourselves. Instead, let's cut a new mental pathway and embrace the many opportunities to grow provided by the people around us.

It's like nature—sometimes we just have to stop and take a good long look around us at the physical beauty of this world. When it comes to people, let's do the same thing. Let's free ourselves—and everyone around us—by taking on the role of the continual learner and grabbing all the lessons we can learn.

There's a lot of free learning available out there! Yes, a few folks may provide lessons of what not to do ("Wow—note to self: Don't ever do that!"). But if we have the right perspective, we can grow every day. Comparison with the right attitude could be your new best friend.

8

Crossing the Street

~c◯:う〜

I f you live in the sticks, you can skip this chapter. But if you live in any place between a small town and Manhattan, this one's for you.

Crossing the street shouldn't be related to how you feel about yourself. It's amazing what people with a low self-image will do to feel better about themselves. I've seen people walk across the street with a look on their faces that says, "I'm walking here, and you drivers have to sit there while I take my sweet time crossing."

To them I have a message: get a life. If the only thing you can do to feel good about yourself has to do with

If the only thing you can do
to feel good about yourself has
to do with crossing the street,
find another source of feeling good
about yourself that's less dangerous
to you and others.

crossing the street, find another source of feeling good about yourself that's less dangerous to you and others.

There's a kind of creative tension between two states of mind when you're crossing the street and there are moving cars. One idea is based on the fact that you *can* cross the street—either in a crosswalk, or anywhere that drivers have to stop to let people pass. You should walk confidently, knowing that it's cool to cross when and where you can.

The other idea involves something called *caution*, or the dedication to living long enough to do all the things you want. I live in a college town where I often have to drive through the campus to get where I'm going. There is a crosswalk in the middle that is sometimes empty, but if I time it wrong, the crosswalk is thick with students going in both directions after class. Some of them look quickly and make sure that my car is actually coming to a stop. They may realize that not everyone is familiar with our state's rules about crosswalks, knows enough to stop, or is paying attention. These people tend to live longer, and they don't make the Survival of the Fittest list.

Then there are the ones who don't even bother looking. They are often on cell phones, or in deep face-to-face conversation with friends, and have apparently forgotten that they are entering a pathway for two-ton vehicles sometimes cruising along at life-crushing speed. Perhaps experience has deceived them into thinking they don't have to take a look; after all, they are still alive at this point. That is not confidence. It's being reckless or stupid.

When it's safe to cross, don't hesitate. Just do it. But keep an eye out. It may be allowable for you to cross, but may not be the best time to venture out. Check both ways and make sure the cars are actually stopped. Your family will thank you for it.

9

Driving

⌒◠◠⃘◌⃘◠◠⌒

Here's a big revelation for someone who wants to act like a grown-up: driving is not a matter of personal expression. Of course, in a small way it is, because we each have a style of driving that's based partly on our personality. But driving isn't like writing an essay or creating your Facebook page. Once you bring that car out of the driveway and onto the road, you are part of a much larger world that you need to be aware of, and it's not your world.

When you hit the road, things have to change. It's not about you talking, or you having fun, or you eating or smoking or blowing off steam. Of course you can do all

There are other people on the road,
and none of them is as accommodating
as your mother. Many of them won't
give you the benefit of the doubt,
and they can't read your mind.

those things *while* driving (that last one isn't really recommended). But when you're driving, the number one goal is you getting yourself and your passengers safely to your destination with the full awareness that the roads are filled with other people trying to do the same thing. If you can't make that your top priority behind the wheel, wait until you can, or don't drive at all.

When you are stopped at an intersection, keep your eye on the light so that when it changes, you're ready to move. No one wants to hear a horn, and no one wants to wait for a light any longer than they have to. So either pause the conversation for a moment, or move your primary attention to the light so that you keep things moving.

Remember that there are other people on the road, and none of them is as accommodating as your mother. Many of them won't give you the benefit of the doubt, and they can't read your mind. So do things like signal in plenty of time before turning. Don't do that weird "veer a little to the right when you're taking a left" thing. And if you can avoid a backup of twenty cars behind you by doing something smart, do it.

Seat belts should be worn whenever you're in a car. In some states, it's the law, and that should be enough. But even if it's not, wear one and make everyone else in your car wear one. Being a grown-up means recognizing that you are part of a family or a group of friends. The people in your life don't want you to die, and wearing a seat belt is one of the best things you can do to make sure that doesn't happen. Maybe you've heard a story of someone who was saved in an accident because he or she was thrown from the vehicle. But there are many *more* stories about people who died because they didn't wear a seat belt. It's not about convenience or some weird definition of being cool. It's about you realizing that you're safer wearing one, and that may be the best thing you ever do for the people who love you.

Avoid distractions when you're driving. In my state, it's illegal to talk on the phone without a hands-free device (though on any day I see a good half-dozen drivers talking away without even trying to hide it—and I don't drive a lot).

The principle behind the law is important. Distracted driving can be dangerous. A few years ago, our area lost five lovely young girls in a tragic car accident.

Investigators discovered that the driver's cell phone was sending a message right before the accident—they don't know whether the driver was the one sending the message. But here's the point: keep your priorities straight when you're responsible for a weighty vehicle hurling through space at seventy miles an hour.

When you're driving, driving needs to be your priority. Talking is great, and pointing and eating and drinking your Mountain Dew can be fun too. But driving has to come first when you're driving. No one can do multiple things at once and do them all well. Be a second-rate contributor to the conversation—but a good driver first.

Making the Car Stop

Maybe *you* know that you're going to stop. But when you slam on your brakes seven feet before coming to a corner, you're sending out a strong suggestion that you're not paying much attention, or that you decided too late to hit the brakes. People tend to freak out at that. If they are walking, they're going to hesitate, or jump out of the way, or get mad and say bad things at you. If they get mad, you probably deserve it.

But the bigger danger when you don't brake in time is that drivers in the road you're coming to tend to not want to get hit, and they may veer to avoid you. That's not a happy thing for drivers in the other lane, or for passengers who don't like getting jerked around.

It's hard to hear sometimes, but statistics show that young drivers have a disproportionately high number of accidents, especially fatal ones. Just check any website for more details. But here are a few eye-openers:

- Motor vehicle accidents are the leading cause of death for U.S. teens.[1]

- Per mile driven, drivers ages sixteen to nineteen are three times more likely than drivers twenty and older to be in a fatal crash.[2]

- Young people ages fifteen to twenty-four represent only 14 percent of the US population. But they account for 30 percent ($19 billion) of the total costs of motor vehicle injuries among males and 28 percent ($7 billion) of the total costs of motor vehicle injuries among females.[3]

I hate to sound like Yoda of *Star Wars* fame, but "Search your feelings—you know it to be true." Young drivers aren't as experienced as older drivers, and that inexperience has caused a lot of accidents. Too many young drivers die because of inexperience.

It's not your fault you haven't been driving for years, and it's not a criticism to say you're inexperienced. But it's stupid to assume that you can have the benefits of experience without the actual experience. Be extra careful those first few years. Take more time, and stay more focused. Death or permanent injury is heartbreaking, whether it's you or other people because of you.

If you're still a bad driver after a few years of driving, then I guess there are other issues that need to be addressed.

Something a little dark happens to
our souls when we go from being
grateful to expecting things.
It can make even the most polished,
articulate adult turn into a polished,
articulate baby.

10

Entitlement

⌒ᴄᴄᴑᴖᴐᴑ⌒

Entitlement is a strange thing. The more grown up you become, the more you realize you aren't entitled to anything. In the United States of America, citizens are entitled to life, liberty, and the chance to pursue being happy. That's a lot, and we should be content with it.

As we mature, we get a bigger picture of life. What we learn when we grow up blends into a larger picture that includes things like how other people grow up, how life is lived in other countries, how life was lived in other times, and how our own new experiences color the way we think and feel about things. We come to realize that our life is vastly different from other people's lives, and a mature attitude on that leads to gratitude most of the time.

Children, on the other hand, feel entitled pretty much from the womb. They feel they have the right to many things—food, their parents' attention, their older sibling's toy, etc. Everyone is basically cool with that and we all secretly hope and believe that they will grow out of it.

Some do; others don't. But the bottom line is this: you weren't entitled to all the things that people freely gave you when you were a kid; you were blessed with them. That's different. And that was then; this is now. Don't stay a child when it comes to feeling entitled. Just because you received something back then doesn't mean that you deserve to keep receiving it now.

If you're still getting those things and you're grateful, good for you! But this doesn't last forever, nor should it. If you're receiving them and you're not grateful—not good. If you're not getting what you think you're entitled to, then work for it, whether it's a car, less interference in your life, or personal respect.

This next thought is a tough one to get. There are many entitlements that we simply expect to get and that expectation can cause problems. For example, some people feel that their parents owe them an inheritance.

Inheritances are great. But parents can do what they want with their money.

If someone has always done something for you, you might feel entitled to continue receiving it. But you're not. You just got used to it. If someone didn't prepare you for not receiving it anymore, that's too bad, but it's never too late to adjust your expectations.

We have many privileges as humans, Americans, employees, workers, etc., and we should enjoy those privileges. But something a little dark happens to our souls when we go from being grateful to expecting things. It can make even the most polished, articulate adult turn into a polished, articulate baby. In the quiet places of all our hearts, let's agree, finally, that what we have is either earned or it's a gift.

You don't have to live your
life in the electronic spotlight.
You can still be a part of it, but you
keep your best thoughts to yourself,
or save them for the disappearing art
of intelligent, personal conversation.

11

Facebook, etc.

~c◌⦚◌⦚⦚⌐

Facebook is a great way to get information out and to connect with friends around the world. Connection is fun, but there are several possible dangers.

The most obvious one is personal. Creepy people get into online groups to see who is stupid or naïve enough to put sensitive information on their wall or website. These bad guys can put together seemingly random bits of personal information and figure out where you live, where you go to school, and when you might be alone. Or they can start the Internet lying thing and drag you into a phony relationship. That's the worst possible scenario, but God knows it's happened.

There's another danger, a more subtle but perilous one. Over time, social media sites can pull you into a kind of exhibitionist way of living. Some people think that everyone cares about what they think and needs to know everything they're doing at all times. These people are called bores.

Some thoughts:

Don't join every "club" or sub-group you're invited to. Most people who use these kinds of sites know that, but too many still get drawn (or guilted) in.

You don't have to tell the world how you feel about Mondays, or how unfair your teacher is, or that you're not happy about the zit on your chin. TMI, really. You know how silly it seems when old people sit around and talk about their medical problems and aches and pains? This is just the younger, electronic version of the same thing.

Remember that every comment you write can be read by everyone, not just those you have in mind when you write it. Every picture you post, every snarky thing that's said are reasons for your parents and school administrators and future employers to 1) ground you, 2) kick you out of school or off a team, or 3) decide not to hire you.

A single stupid comment can take you out of the running for a great job. And you'll never know about it.

You don't have to live your life in the electronic spotlight. You can still be a part of it, but you should keep your best thoughts to yourself, or save them for the disappearing art of intelligent, personal conversation. Living life even partially in public is only good for celebrities and people making money from Facebook. It can get you in trouble or limit your future. It can also trick you into thinking that in the real world, your opinions and judgments and complaints about every little thing are something people out there really care about. Unless they love you, they generally don't, and that's a healthy thing.

Be honest. Do you want to be spoiled and taken care of? If you answer yes, go back to the end of the line and tell your parents they have more work to do with you.

12

Financial Independence

~⊂◌⦂◌⊃~

You're really a grown-up when you're independent from your parents. That means you buy your own food, pay for the roof over your head, buy your own clothes, and pay for your own transportation. If you live with your parents, almost-independence is paying them rent, contributing to the food bill, doing your own laundry (or finding a way to give back to Mom for doing it for you), and paying for your own transportation (gas, insurance, subway/bus cards or tokens). It also means finding out what Mom and Dad want from you, and giving it to them on time and without attitude.

But real, honest-to-God financial independence (FI) is supporting yourself completely. When you have your own place, do your own shopping and laundry, pay all your own bills, and don't regularly lean on anyone for anything, that's real independence. Otherwise, it's either a step along the way, a trial run of "almost there," or somebody's fooling themselves.

You begin the process of acting like a grown-up in terms of money when you actually *want* to be financially independent. When you see financial independence as a good thing—even if it's a little scary—that's step one.

Be honest. Do you want to be spoiled and taken care of? If you answer yes, go back to the end of the line and tell your parents they have more work to do with you. Life doesn't work like that, and you really shouldn't be allowed out on your own yet.

If you want to be independent at thirteen so you can do what you want with no restrictions, you're either sad or being silly. If you think acting like a grown-up means having no restrictions, then you need to go back to the line (the middle this time, not the end) and take another good hard look at any grown-up's life. You have some major clues to get before moving ahead.

If you want to be independent because things are seriously wrong at home and you want to get out, you need help, not independence. Look for the assistance of a trusted adult relative, religious leader, or teacher. Financial independence won't solve that kind of problem.

But if you want to be independent because it's the mature and healthy thing to do, and you realize that with the joy of independence comes a variety of responsibilities (and you're willing to take them on), then go to the head of the line. You probably don't know what you're getting into yet, but at least you have some sense of where you want to go.

Once you've decided to move toward financial independence for the right reasons, let time be your friend. There's no need to rush things. You should be able to look back and see some real progress over time, even if it's not what you want yet. You should also be able to look ahead and see the opportunities for more independence, and you should be working on that with your parents. Taking on more and more responsibility with money is what true FI is all about.

Make moves toward FI along with the normal milestones: graduation from high school or college, or getting that first job that puts money in your pocket. When your financial picture gets better, you should be contributing something somewhere.

What big goals do you and your parents see for you? Training for a good job? College? Getting those things behind you becomes a stepping-stone into greater levels of financial independence.

How do your parents see you becoming financially independent? If you don't know, ask. You might be surprised at the answer. Even if they don't quite know yet, asking the question is a great start. When you're ready, tell them you'd like to work with their expectations and plans for you, even if those things aren't completely clear in your own mind yet.

One sign of acting like a grown-up is recognizing where you are in this journey, and moving along in a way that works for everyone.

13

Finish What You Start

❧⟳⟲❧

Don't start anything you don't intend to finish. Don't waste time, energy, and resources by starting something you're not going to complete. Being aimless is not good for you or the environment.

But there's another reason that is just as important. Determining to finish whatever you start will affect the way you go about doing whatever it is you're doing. It's like tennis. In tennis, planning your follow-through from the beginning affects the *whole swing*. If you have the end in mind from the start of something, you'll have a more focused, dedicated, and smoother approach throughout. What works for tennis swings also works for college, finding a career, becoming a billionaire, and marriage.

Don't waste time, energy, and
resources by starting something
you're not going to complete.

"Do or do not. There is no *try*." That's one of the few things from *Star Wars* that I can quote and actually mean. While I appreciate Yoda's warning about living a life of hesitance, I would go a step further. Don't just *do it*. Right from the start, get a clear picture in your heart and mind of what the end looks like. That will change everything about how you do it.

What if you just want to experiment? The same thing applies. Consider why you're doing the experiment. What do you want to learn when you're done?

Developing a habit of finishing what you start will bring a higher level of focus and dedication to whatever task you're beginning. That will improve the likelihood that you'll actually finish, you'll do a better job throughout the process, and you'll get a lot more out of it in the end.

It's OK to relate intelligently to
your teachers. Don't brownnose,
but if you're having trouble
with something, ask for help.

14

Going to Class,
Part One—High School

~cↄↄↄↄ~

Y̶ou pretty much have to go to high school. And the peer pressure to act in less-than-grown-up ways is intense. So while it's not impossible to act like a grown-up in high school, it's really hard. For one thing, you're too young to have enough perspective to look *back* over your life (all fifteen-or-so years of it!) and figure out how to act like a mature student; there's just not much "looking back" available to work with when you're in high school.

Every class level is different, and most of a student's energy goes into figuring out the differences and making adjustments. Plus, you're growing so fast—physically, intellectually, emotionally—that there's little time to stop and consider how much more mature you are now than last year. You just go with the flow. And by the time you get to the end of the road—being a graduating senior— you're so happy to get out and get on with your life that you don't want to look back in any way.

But for the rare student who really wants to get as much as he or she can out of high school, here goes.

Don't try to be popular with everyone—you can't. Find other students who share your values. Form various levels of friendship: some good, close friends; several acquaintances; lots of folks you know a little about. Whenever you interact with people, be as nice and as real as you can. Learn how be a good friend yourself.

It's OK to relate intelligently to your teachers. Don't brownnose, but if you're having trouble with something, ask for help. If you get a good answer, you'll be ahead. If you get a brush-off, at least *you* acted like a grown-up. And you'll get a jump on the art of relating to people in power.

It may be more than a coincidence that "hell" and "high school" begin with the letter h. But you don't have to be like almost everyone else and just try to get through it. Learn how to be a good friend, make a few friends yourself, and get a jump on relating to different kinds of people. Your heart won't forget these things, even if your brain forgets nearly everything else.

Being the best student you can be
will provide you with life lessons and
character traits that will serve you
well in the real world.

15

Going to Class,
Part Two—College

⌐ᴄᴏᴉᴐᴐ⌐

College is completely different from high school, so the rules—and the recommendations—are different.

First suggestion: Go to class. Well, duh! No, not duh. Lots of students don't go, especially toward the end of the semester. That will either hurt you or make the professor ticked, or both. As a professor, I don't take it personally if a student skips class, but I know how much the students miss when they blow off class. It always hurts them when it comes to quizzes and tests, and ends up damaging their final grade.

I understand the pressure at the end of a semester, and how much time is needed for projects and papers. But going to class is the most effective use of your time. Make it a priority and let other nonacademic things slide. The time is there—just figure it out.

When you go to class, *be* in class. And let your professor see you.

If you sit toward the front, your professors might think you're hard of hearing or even deaf (which is literally the case sometimes where I teach). But they'll probably assume that you actually want to learn. Sitting in the middle of the room indicates that you're kind of interested, but giving yourself the option to disengage. If you sit in the back rows, it conveys that you 1) don't care about the class, 2) want to sleep or go to your happy place quite often, or 3) intend to talk the whole time. This is the best way to signal to your professor that you're not interested.

Do not do these things:

Surf the web during class. It's really rude. Plus, you can't surf and learn at the same time. And it can be very distracting to those around you.

Text in class. It's really rude. Plus you can't text and learn at the same time.

Talk at a good level of volume once class starts. It's really rude, and you can't talk and learn at the same time. (Sensing a pattern here?)

Keep giving your professors the same excuses about how busy you are and why you can't get your work done on time. They're probably at least as busy as you are, and they understand how much time students dedicate to extracurricular activities. We all have the same twenty-four hours in the day. Others are getting their work done on time, so you probably can too. It's usually just a matter of setting priorities.

Do these things:

Keep your prof in the loop about things that seriously affect your work. I have a rather large class, and at least one person a semester loses a grandparent. Sad but true. Having them tell me that they are traveling out of town and why makes me sympathetic and makes me want to give them every break I can. When students have some kind of emergency, letting me know ASAP makes me respect their sense of maturity. Hearing from a student days after they don't show up in class also sends a message. Not a good one.

Let your profs know when you're struggling with something. The best time to do this is not the day before something is due. This sends the message that you are an irritant. Don't do that. Nothing makes me happier as a professor than when students ask for help in a way that shows they have actually started working on the paper or project in question.

Learn how time can be your friend. It seems like we consider time our enemy in this culture, and having lots of deadlines in your college life can make it seem that way for you as a student. But you don't have to work *against* deadlines. You can work *with* them.

Try this, and you'll give yourself a big break and find your papers and projects a lot easier over the long run.

First, take the project or paper and break it into parts. What decisions do you need to make first? Make 'em! Honestly, the hardest part is deciding what you're going to write about, or what angle you're going to take on a project.

It's fun to delay that sort of thing, but really, it hurts you. Decide on the topic, and your approach to the project, then do the first few things that need to be done. For my class on film, the students first have to decide what film to see and what element to analyze (such as lighting, color, editing, sound, camera movement, etc.). I urge them to decide those things quickly, and watch the film with that particular element in mind. Then I tell them to go on to other things for a few days, or longer. While they're doing other things, their subconscious minds start putting the paper together.

Try it yourself. Get an early start on a paper sometime, take a break, and then revisit it. The paper will be half-written in your brain, and you'll end up writing a deeper, richer paper. If you wait until the last minute, you may pull off an impressive feat of doing a late night or an all-nighter, but your paper will be more shallow and you won't have learned as much. (It's like cramming for a test. What gets slammed into the brain at the last minute doesn't tend to stick after the test.)

Being a college student isn't anyone's final goal. But it's good preparation for life. Being the best student you can be will provide you with life lessons and character traits that will serve you well in the real world. You are going to need all the help you can out there, so you might as well get everything you can out of your college experience.

16

Interviewing for a Job

There are a lot of good sources for how to conduct a job interview. I only want to speak to the way you might choose to dress for the occasion.

First, don't go to an interview in your everyday clothes (unless you are specifically asked to). Some folks want to be seen for who they really are, so they come to the interview with green hair, facial tattoos, ear-nose-and-throat rings, and clothing that reflects the raging of man against the machine.

This kind of outfit actually gets in the way of interviewers seeing who you are. To connect with you, they need to have eye contact. If you're a walking collage of styles and colors, your clothes will be a distraction. You're only being true to yourself if you dress in a manner that helps the person see who you are. If you think you can only express who you really are by your clothing, hair, and piercings, maybe you're not ready for steady employment.

17

Investing

～ ⌒⊙!⊙⌒ ～

We all know the basic rules about investing financially: you have money, you invest it, and if it
makes more money for you, you keep putting more
money in. If an investment doesn't work out, you take
your money out.

Yet apart from money, we're still all investors. We invest
time, we invest energy, and we invest our hearts. Some
investments will turn out better than others. College, for
example, is generally a good investment if you're serious
about it. Business or skills training is also a good investment of time and money. Investing time and heart into
a good friendship is almost always a good investment.

Don't let stubbornness or wishful thinking make you keep investing when you can tell it's a losing proposition. It's painful to be disappointed, but it's stupid to pretend things are different from what they are.

Time

You may feel like you have all the time in the world, but you don't. It feels like you have a lot when you're young, and that's important, because you usually need the sense of having a lot so you have the freedom and courage to do what you need to.

Time is like money in some ways. But unlike money, no matter how well we invest our time, we all end up with less of it than we had at the start. Don't be driven, but consider time precious and spend it wisely.

Heart investments are the trickiest, because they're more personal and more dangerous. Happily, some don't matter all that much. When we're young, for example, we invest our hearts and minds without realizing we're doing it. We root for baseball or football teams because our friends or parents do. I am a Yankees fan (don't hate me) because my dad was. I root for my local NFL team, even though rooting for them makes me well acquainted with constant disappointment. Investments like this are real, but ultimately not that important. They usually just result in being either happy or bummed out for a day when your team loses.

It's when you get to friends and other more serious relationships that you make the most worthwhile and risky investments. If you're going to have a serious relationship with someone, you have to invest time and energy and heart in it. If it turns out to be a good investment, keep enjoying the relationship.

But if your friend turns into a bad friend or even a bad influence, stop investing. Don't kick yourself for getting into the relationship unless you knew better back then. Maybe you were right to give things a try. But don't let stubbornness or wishful thinking make you keep investing when you can tell it's a losing proposition. It's painful to be disappointed, but it's stupid to pretend things are different from what they are.

If a potential love relationship goes bad, stop investing in it. Don't let butt-headed pride prevent you from admitting that you might have made a mistake. It may have been a good investment in the beginning. But if things go south and you can't trust the person anymore, stop investing. And if you can look back and learn something that will prevent you from making the same mistake in the future, grab that lesson!

The Other Half of Investing

When investing is over, you need to make an emotional and mental *divestment*—like taking your money out after a bad financial investment. After your head stops spinning and your heart stops aching, take some serious time to rethink things. Dump old thoughts and attitudes. Give your heart time to stop hurting, then recalibrate it to a better and healthier place. Talk things out with someone who knows more than you do. And don't invest again too quickly. (If you're the kind of person who always has to have a boyfriend or girlfriend, this is a good time to divest your thoughts on the matter.)

You're going to make a lot of investments without even thinking about it. Some won't matter much, like which store you like best or what TV shows you want to watch. But sometimes we paint ourselves into a corner with our more serious investments, and when things don't turn out, we feel like we have to keep investing simply because we've invested so much already. That's a trap— don't get caught in it.

You *will* make some bad investments. It's called living. But don't let your pain or your pride cause you to keep investing. People who never learn from their mistakes tend to make the same ones over and over. Don't be that person.

18

Invitations

~c꜀⁙ꙅꙕ~

I f you get an invitation that doesn't say anything about responding, you're off the hook. Just go or don't go. If it says, "Regrets only," you only have to contact the person if you're not planning to go.

If it says, "RSVP," you have to respond. RSVP means "*Répondez, s'il vous plaît*," which is French for "please respond." So whether you decide to go or not, you have to let the person know. This shows that you're not a self-centered jerk. And it will be helpful to the person holding the party.

If you don't see the words "and guest" following your name, come alone. Do not bring a friend, your new girlfriend, your cousin, or your child. It's only one event—you'll live.

The first half of acting like an adult
is seeing that there are a lot of systems
out there; the second half is doing
your part in the system.

19

It's Not About You

⌐c◠◡◦◡◠⌐

When you move from being a kid to being a grown-up—no matter when that happens—a momentous event occurs: you realize you are not the center of the universe. And that's good. When you're with others, when you drive, when you walk into a store, you're entering something bigger than yourself.

I'm not talking about the big questions, like "Who am I and why am I here?" We're talking about the little things. When you take the car out, you're part of a system of roads, drivers, other cars, and laws that you have to fit into. If you take the subway or a bus, you find out quickly that you're a part of a larger system over which you have very little control.

Being a grown-up is realizing that and being OK with it. Being immature means thinking that every law, every driver, every delayed bus or subway car is against you and your plans. Acting like a grown-up is understanding that you have to work with the roads in front of you, the people on those roads, the other subway passengers, and that really, no one is out to get you. You accept the other drivers on the road, or you can see that one late subway car or bus affects the whole system, not just you.

When you go to the store, it's not just about you buying what you want and getting out of there. If that happens, great. If not, don't take it personally. Maybe the store is out of something, or the less-than-helpful cashier just lost a friend. Or there was a hard winter that made your item more expensive. If that's the case, sorry. But it's still not personal.

The first half of acting like an adult is seeing that there are a lot of systems out there; the second half is doing your part in whatever system you find yourself.

It's a good sign when you realize the world doesn't revolve around you and what you want. I'm not going to challenge you not to be a selfish pig—you can go ahead and be one if you want. But you don't have to act like one.

The first big mistake with love
is not giving yourself the gift of time.
You may feel impatient, which is OK—
unless you act on it.

20

Love

⁓⌒◠◠◠⌒⁓

When it comes to love, we all have our own per-spectives and experiences. Here's the bottom line, though: Love is about the other person, not about you. Love means putting others first, trying to meet their needs, and wanting the best for them. If all you talk about is how you feel, you're not dealing with love yet. When you think in terms of "us" and begin to focus on your beloved, you're on your way.

What love is not:

Love is not just a feeling. Real love has lots of emotions, and they can be the most wonderful feelings of your life. But love is more than feelings. If you take your advice from Disney movies and "follow your heart," it can be the worst trip of your life.

Love is not thinking of being with the other person all the time. That's the "I" word—infatuation. Sorry. Most people don't want to hear that word; it feels like someone isn't validating their feelings. Let me validate your feelings. They're real. In fact, infatuation is a roller-coaster ride of emotions. It may even be the first stage in a relationship that leads to love. It's just too early in the process to know. Our mistake isn't having the feelings—it's misnaming them.

The first big mistake with love is not giving yourself the gift of time. You may feel impatient, which is OK—unless you act on it. Acting out of impatience sets you up for trouble. If you really believe you're in love, test it. I don't mean saying something stupid like "If you love me, you'll ..." That's not a true test—it's just insecurity or manipulation.

People used to test metals by putting them in a fire or subjecting them to intense heat so the impurities rise to the top. The final result is a metal with fewer imperfections.

To test a relationship, don't give it heat; give it time. Time weeds out the junk in whatever we're calling love. It weeds out infatuation. It weeds out wanting a boyfriend or girlfriend just to have someone to do things with on the weekend, or just because you want to be a part of a couple. It weeds out the new, the fresh, and the different because none of those things can last. When you think you might be in love, time can be your best friend.

If you're resisting that, ask yourself, *What's the problem in waiting?* We sometimes turn into brats and start whining when we hear this question. OK, go ahead and whine for a minute, or a weekend. But then grow up, and stop wanting everything now. Whatever you *can* get right now is probably not what you're going to want over the long haul. The only thing bad about waiting is that your patience is tested and you can't have the life you want right this minute.

You may think a new relationship will last forever against all odds. Letting things develop takes love out of your imagination (where things are perfect and untouched by the challenges of life) and puts it into reality. Reality includes work, tiredness, families and friends, sickness, inconveniences, grouchy moods, coughs and snotty noses—yours or theirs. Real love will survive all those. In fact, love will prosper and deepen. If real life threatens your "love," it's not real love.

I've watched many people fall in love and get married. I don't know one couple who took their time in the relationship and lived to regret it. Yet everyone I know who rushed into a serious relationship or marriage has regretted it, sometimes terribly so.

The Wonderful Rule of Threes

There are no guarantees in love. But here's a rule that's of great help to people in love. If your family (parents, siblings, closest relatives, etc.), your friends, and the adviser who knows you best (counselor, minister, mentor) all agree that this is a good relationship, that's an excellent indicator that you should probably keep pursuing it. If any of them has a problem with the relationship, find out why.

When you do, make it easy for them to tell you what they really think. Create an environment that allows them to tell you the truth. Be open to what they share with you, and don't throw their words back in their faces.

Acknowledge that they care for you enough to be honest, and wrestle your feelings through until you're grateful for that, even if you don't like what you're hearing. Listen closely to what they say, because your future peace and happiness may depend on it.

Having the OK from one of these groups isn't enough. Your relatives don't see you and your "loved one" the same way your friends do. Or maybe your relatives are the only ones who see the things you don't. People in these three groups will all have different ways of giving you a much-needed reality check, because they each have different perspectives and concerns. If your relationship gets an honest thumbs-up from everyone, that's an excellent start.

Love is a special thing. Just don't call something *love* too early. Make time work for you and listen, listen, listen to what others say. Some cynics don't think it's even possible to be smart about something like love. I disagree. Giving love time and taking input seriously are investments in the health of your relationship, and one of the best gifts you could give yourself and your future.

The truest sign of maturity
is the ability to delay gratification.
That's especially true with marriage.
But you're not really delaying
gratification—in the long run,
you're increasing it.

21

Marriage

⌐co:ᴐ⌐

Marriage is great. Not everyone does it well, but it's still a fabulous idea. It's also the foundation of our society.

There are many things that can be said about being married. I only have two things to say here.

Marriage is not just a declaration of love, no matter how genuine. It's a commitment. (Check out the chapter "Finish What You Start.") If you're committed to making it through until death, you will add an ingredient to your marriage that living together—or thinking that divorce is a backdoor option—can never give you. It will take you through the rough times. Surviving rough times brings perspective and wisdom. And you're gonna need those in marriage!

If you can't see spending the rest of your life with this person, don't get married. At least not yet. Commit when you're genuinely ready to. Commitment keeps love alive, even through the times when you don't feel the love. Feelings come and go. A commitment allows love to come flowering back after the hard times.

Here's my second recommendation. And no, I'm not crazy: don't get married until you can afford it. Just because you're in love doesn't mean you're ready to be married. It's best not to have to lean on anyone besides each other for creating and sustaining your new household.

Some people think two can live as cheaply as one. That's, to be kind, dumb. Believing that is an indicator that you're living in unreality and should hold off awhile.

Other folks are just impatient. They want to get married to 1) have sex or have it more regularly, 2) finally live together, 3) be away from parents, or 4) be part of a romantic dream.

Marriage

We live in a selfish age, and we are told we should get what we want as soon as we want. That's a terrible way to approach marriage. Marriage is two people blending their lives, and that needs a solid financial foundation to work well. When you get married, form a household. Live on your own, and pay all your own bills.

Money and how to use it wisely are important issues for every couple. Starting with a solid financial foundation is one of the best gifts you can give to the person you're marrying.

Premarital counseling—do it! I know many people who sought premarital counseling and are happy they did. They went into their marriages more prepared to handle the inevitable difficulties and challenges. If you can avail yourself of some, you'll be doing yourself a big favor.

Wait until you can be your own family and survive as a unit on your own. If that means finishing school first, do it. If it means establishing your career first, do it. If it means saving some money and developing some financial goals, do that. The greatest wedding gifts you can give to each other are love and commitment. But right after that comes an independent and financially stable base.

The truest sign of maturity is the ability to delay gratification. That's especially true with marriage. But you're not just delaying gratification—in the long run, you're increasing it.

22

Meeting People

~c○!つ~

Meeting people is simple, but not always easy—especially if you're shy. It's composed of two simple steps: greet and connect.

Greeting is easy. Just say something. If you shake the person's hand, don't do the limp-fish thing. Use a strong, solid handshake. Find a way of verbally greeting people that works for you and make the person you're meeting comfortable. And at the risk of sounding like your mother, don't mumble.

Connecting is where we get outside of ourselves. For just one moment, it's not about you, but about the person you're meeting. Look people in the eye while you're talking to them, whether you're shaking hands or just giving a quick hello from across the room. Even if it's quick, do what you can to make the connection comfortable and real. It may be a stretch for you, but you'll be glad you did it.

23

Money and College

~co:oc~

Here's the big thing about college loans: you have to pay them back. And that can either hamper or cripple your future for a long time. Think, think, think about how much you feel you can borrow, and consider your options.

You don't have to go to an expensive four-year school. You can get your associate's degree from a less expensive two-year college and save a bundle. Then you can transfer. It may not be as fun for you now, but life will be a lot more fun later when you're not paying the equivalent of two mortgage or rent payments every month.

This isn't fun, either, but it might be smart: work for a year or two, and then go to college. Or get that associate's degree, work for a while again, and then complete your education. The only word of warning here is to make sure you actually get that education. Don't let a little bit of freedom and spending money seduce you into thinking that you should just keep working and go for the immediate satisfaction of having more money than you've ever had in your pocket. Do a little research on the financial benefits of finishing high school and then all the various levels of college. You'll be surprised and encouraged.

Unless you have a family business or a great skill that translates into a solid career, it's usually worth going to college. It's just not worth taking out tens of thousands of dollars in loans and mortgaging your future if you can avoid it.

24

Owning Your Youth

~⚬⦂⚬~

The most mature thing young people can do is *own* the fact that they're young. Don't resist it. Embrace all there is to being young—limitations and all.

Look at it from the other side for a moment. When old people dress and act like they're young, it's kind of embarrassing. And when half-blind eighty-eight-year-olds drive like they think they're twenty-five, it's dangerous.

Well, switch that around. If you're young, don't pretend you're not. Trying to act older is as crazy as your best friend's mother dressing like a teenager. It might seem cool for a little while, but in the long run it's embarrassing.

If you're young,
you don't have to wait to get old
to get wisdom.

I loved the movie *Juno*. It was filled with great one-liners, but my favorite was when Juno came home and her father asked where she'd been and what she was doing. She said, "Out dealing with things way beyond my maturity level." That's a pretty grown-up statement. It says you're humble enough to know that you can't handle what's going on, but also shows the realization that in a few years, you'll be better at dealing with your problems than you are now.

Looking Ahead

The best way to own your youth is to be happy with whatever age you are and still be looking forward to the next milestone in your life. Too many kids under ten can't wait to be "double digits." Preteens want to be sixteen, then eighteen, then twenty, then twenty-one. At twenty-five they have their eye on cheaper car insurance. But then people hit thirty, and many freak out. Some save their freaking out for thirty-nine, forty, or fifty. Then they start looking at retirement and they have something to look forward to again, so the incessant marching of time doesn't seem so dreadful anymore. But they don't look forward to their next birthday like when they were teenagers. They either practice the art of denial, or they get bitter about it.

Try to be content with the age you are. The most enjoyable folks to be around are those who find every age cool because they enjoy the benefits that every age brings. That wonderful perspective comes with wisdom, which sometimes comes with age. But if you're young, you don't have to wait to get old to get wisdom.

When you're young, there are a lot of things you can't do. And some things you can do, but you aren't particularly good at yet. That's OK. You don't have to apologize for being young. But we all have to apologize for acting stupid. And one of the stupidest things people can do is to not act their age.

When my dad turned fifty-five, he told me that he was going to attend a driving class. My father was a good driver, so I was curious about why he wanted to take the course. He said that one reason was a break in insurance rates. The better reason was that he realized that his reflexes weren't what they were when he was younger, and he wanted to take the course to see how he could compensate for that loss. I thought that was pretty smart.

When you're eighteen and you look back at when you were fourteen, it's like you were a whole different person. Some folks get all heady and dizzy at eighteen because they've changed so much so fast, and they're smarter than they've ever been. And that's true. But when you're twenty-one, your eighteen-year-old self may seem like kind of a jerk. This process will keep going on until you're twenty-five or so, and then it slows down. The smart you of today will eventually morph into the not-all-that-bright you of yesterday.

The best thing you can do is get some perspective on the whole aging process. Don't be too impressed with your current self, because your future self is going to be even smarter than you are now.

Here are some of the things younger people often have problems with:

- Knowing how much they can drink before getting silly, then dumb, then dangerous to themselves, then dangerous to others.

- Knowing how any school, group, or company really works. (You won't understand that until you've been hanging around for a while.)

- Thinking they know more than most people who are older. (Some older folks aren't so bright, but experience does count for something.)

- Thinking they already know who they are. (Most people keep growing well into their twenties, and that involves a lot of changing. Be humble—parts of the brain keep growing until age twenty-five.)

It's OK to acknowledge that you're not very experienced. That's not a criticism. I'm not very experienced in a lot of areas myself. That's why I go online, or turn to books or friends. Understanding that you only know a few things is smart. Knowing there is much more to learn at any age is one of the smartest things of all.

It's good to think about what you've learned. But it's also good to realize that there's a lot you don't know yet.

25

Sexuality

~⊂◌⊃~

Being in the film and music industry, I have seen many young, talented singers, dancers, and actors suddenly discover that they were becoming sexual beings. Soon they started exposing their bodies, taking "daring" film roles, and singing about things that seemed designed to prove to the world that their hormones had kicked in. This is acting like a … well, it's not acting like a grown-up.

Your sexuality is yours. It doesn't belong to the world. And becoming a sexual being only proves that you're getting older. You don't have to prove you're growing up by demonstrating to the public that you're physically mature enough to reproduce.

You are not your body;
you just have your body.
Know the difference.

Parading your grown-up body is not only immature, it could also be dangerous to ever acting like a grown-up. You are not your body; you just *have* your body. Know the difference. There's nothing sadder than someone who doesn't get that. (Just check out half of the reality shows on TV. But just for a minute—you lose brain cells with every second of viewing.)

When the hormones kick in, you change so fast you can get dizzy. You want people to know you're growing up, and it seems like the most dramatic statement you can make is to use your sexuality to demonstrate that. But that shows that you're struggling to grow up, not that you've arrived.

Your sexuality, once it kicks in, will be a part of you the rest of your life. You'll have to learn how to express it, how to tame it, how to aim it properly, and how to make it a part of your personality. You don't have to act like a sexual being all the time just because you are. All those people that don't flaunt their sexuality—they're sexual beings too. They just wear it on the inside, not on the outside.

Becoming a physically sexual being is a stage. That doesn't mean it's not real or powerful. But it won't always be like that—or feel like that. The important thing is not to do anything rash or hurtful while you're in that stage.

Danger, Danger

Your sexuality is one of the most powerful parts of you. It can help you or break you. Let's say you become a professional athlete, and you have sex with lots of women, and some of them end up having your babies. You might make really good money for ten or fifteen years, but it'll all go for child support. And would you really want to be one of those kids? This kind of person doesn't know what to do with his sexuality, so he ends up hurting himself and a lot of other people.

And don't believe what movies and TV show. Having sex leads to pregnancy. No one's discovered a 100 percent effective contraceptive. In movies, it's funny when a person gets pregnant and someone else asks, "How did that happen?" It's not so funny in real life.

My wife and I have a name for the single time we didn't try to prevent a pregnancy. That name is Ben (our oldest child). We occasionally joke that his middle name should have been "It'll be OK just this once." We were married at the time. And of course we love him more than words can say. But he was a surprise. This kind of thing happens every day to people who aren't ready to raise a child. Get in front of the curve and realize that in the real world, sex generally leads to more people.

We all have to figure out how to integrate our sexuality into ourselves. And for most people, it's a rough road. There are lots of land mines out there. Your sexuality may come on you on like a tidal wave, but you have to figure out what to do with it, and then make it a part of who you are. Prove you can act like a grown-up by owning it instead of letting it own you.

Suicide is never the right answer,
no matter what's wrong.
It's actually the worst possible choice.

26

Suicide

⌒⊂⊙⌒

As of 2014, suicide was the second leading cause of death for people aged fifteen to twenty-four.[4]

I hope you don't need to read this section for yourself as much as to help others out. If you are considering suicide, please read this and take it seriously. Suicide is never the right answer, no matter what's wrong. It's actually the worst possible choice.

First, let me assure you that things will be better. When you get older, your life gets bigger. You'll understand your problems better and they won't seem as overpowering anymore. Good things will happen, and you'll get some perspective on whatever is so hard now. So give time a chance.

Plus, help is available if you look for it. There is someone out there right now who can help you. If your first attempts at getting help didn't work well, give it another try. Look in different places than before. If you're persistent, you'll find what you need.

If you believe in God, this is a terrible way to meet Him. Whatever thoughts you are having that lead you in the direction of suicide are either lies or partial truths that are all twisted around. Don't believe lies.

Suicide is selfish. It doesn't end the pain—it just transfers it to other people. Suicide only kills you. Your pain lives on, tormenting others, sometimes for the rest of their lives. Find a way to kill the pain, not yourself—preferably by getting to the root of it.

Suicide is a seductive monster in a dark and scary room, calling you inside. Just slam the door in that monster's face and look for a better way out. You'll find it.

27

The Trust Thing

~·c·o:·ɔ·ɔ~

Your parents know you better than you know yourself. They may have forgotten some of the feelings
of being a teenager, but they know your history, and
they're not as forgetful about yesterday as you probably are. So they're a little more cautious about giving
you enough rope to hang yourself, as the expression
goes.

Parents want to feel confident (do you hear me—*feel* it
right down to their toes) that you're not going to hurt
yourself. Just telling them you're trustworthy is worth-
less. But if you show that you can handle a small amount
of responsibility, they'll give you more privileges.

You need to establish a history
of trust. Even if that takes
more time than you'd like.

The Trust Thing

Most of us like to forget about our past and cast our eyes on a rosy future when we're trying to get people to trust us. But your parents are looking at your past at the same time you're looking toward your future. So you need to establish a history of trust they can look at.

My wife and I let our younger son do a lot of things when he was a teenager. He always told us where he was going, and he rarely tried to stretch the rules. When our daughter hit the same age, she got upset when we constantly asked questions about how, what, when, and where. She protested that her older brother got to do those things at a younger age than she was. After a while, our daughter realized that we were not asking so many questions anymore. When she asked her mother about it, she was told that we didn't need to anymore. Without even realizing it, she'd established her own history of trust.

Even if you have to vote for
the lesser of two evils, do it. So it's
not ideal—few things are.
Besides, the older you get, the more
every race looks like a choice between
the lesser of two evils.

28

Voting

I f you don't vote, you lose the right to complain about the world.

People have actually died so you can vote. You should feel grateful for that.

There are very few ways we can contribute politically without going into public service (which is what politics used to be). There is so much corruption and hypocrisy in politics, we may think that one vote doesn't matter. But a single vote can make a big difference. We had a district attorney race in our region in which each candidate got exactly the same number of votes—and we're talking numbers in the thousands!

Even if you have to vote for the lesser of two evils, do it. So it's not ideal—few things are. Besides, the older you get, the more every race looks like a choice between the lesser of two evils.

So either vote or keep your political opinions to yourself.

29

Watching Movies

～⌒⊙⁞⊙⌒～

Watching movies at home is a personal experience. So if you want to talk through the whole thing, that's no big deal. If you, or somebody who's watching with you, missed something important, you can go back and play it again.

But watching a movie in a theater is a group experience— a completely different animal than watching at home. So keep quiet. It's OK to talk quietly during previews. But during the intro credits, close down the conversation. During the movie, a whispered comment here and there is cool. (The public whisper is nearly a lost art. Try to bring it back.) But don't take away from everyone else's

If you let the movie draw you in
and carry you along, you'll have
something worth talking about later.

movie experience. They didn't come to the theater to hear you talk. You can talk your head off after the movie's done.

There is more at stake here than not being rude. Let me put my film professor hat on for a moment. There's something special about letting a film pull you into its images and sounds and themes and colors, and take you on its ride. You can't have that experience if you're talking to your friends the whole time. Let yourself become a member of the audience for a couple of hours. If you let the movie draw you in and carry you along, you'll have something worth talking about later.

Talking isn't the only rude thing you can do while you're watching a movie. If you have to unwrap a piece of candy, cover it with a jacket or at least do it quickly. It is majorly irritating to have someone take forty-seven seconds to slowly undo a candy wrapper—and really distracting.

And please turn off your cell phone. If you are expecting an important call, you probably shouldn't be at a movie theater. If you think you might get an emergency call, put your phone on silent or vibrate and sit in a place where you can leave the theater quickly if you need to speak to someone. Do not carry on a phone conversation in the theater. (Yes, there are people who do that.) Do what they tell fighters in a bar—take it outside.

Texting is almost as bad. If you get a text, the light from your screen will take everyone around you out of the movie experience. If it's that important, leave the theater to read it. Or sit on the floor, put a coat over your head and read it quietly. Really.

30

You're Not a Loser
(Unless You Choose to Be)

Many of us struggle with feeling like losers. By the most common definition, we're all losers because we've all lost some contest or failed to reach a goal. Since we're all going to be losers every so often, we'd better be prepared for that reality.

But losing or failing doesn't make you a loser. And no one is born a loser, like being born with red hair and freckles. What makes you a loser is what you do when things don't go the way you want them to.

Losing or failing doesn't make you a loser. And no one is born a loser, like being born with red hair and freckles. What makes you a loser is what you do when things don't go the way you want them to.

There are two things that make someone a loser. Either they stop trying, or they don't learn from their mistakes.

If you lose at something, it means you're trying. And if you're trying, that means you're not a loser.

Thomas Edison spoke of his many so-called failures before discovering how to make a successful light bulb. He's credited as saying, "I have not failed. I've just found ten thousand ways that won't work." He didn't let failures make him a failure. Another quote of his sheds some light (pun intended) on this thinking. "Many of life's failures are people who did not realize how close they were to success when they gave up."[5] Edison didn't give up. You shouldn't either. You have no idea what might be around the corner.

Edison learned from mistakes. He discovered a lot of valuable information along the way to his eventual goal. He kept learning what didn't work until he discovered what did, and he changed the world. Mistakes are often better teachers than any book we could read or class we could take.

Some people like to say, "I don't regret anything." If that's true, that's a shame. Grown-ups learn from their goof-ups how they hurt someone, what they did wrong, and thoughtless things they said. If by saying, "I don't regret anything," they mean that they don't live in regret, that's great. But some people plow through life never learning a thing from their mistakes. That can seem cool and brave from a distance. But that's being a loser, no matter how "successful" a person may become.

You are the only one who can make yourself a loser. No circumstance or series of failures can make you a loser. The good news is that if you think you've been a loser, you can choose not to be at any time.

Acting like a grown-up takes some work, but it's just about the best thing you can do for yourself and others. It makes life clearer and easier. You become a bigger and better person. Here's a delicious irony in life: the more you step back and lose yourself as you look at the big picture of things, and the more you keep others in mind, the more you become the real you.

And that's worth celebrating.

Acknowledgments

Chris DuPré, brother, author (*The Wild Love of God* and *The Love Project*), and my best friend. I am grateful and honored to be your brother. You are more of a blessing than I can put into words.

Clint Morgan, my nonrelative best friend who graciously provided valuable feedback for this book. The friendship I share with you and Barbara is like an oasis in my life. I love having a dear friend who is so much like me and so very different at the same time.

Bruce Plummer, my other dear friend. You've gone beyond acting like a grown-up. You *are* one, you think like one, and you have a grown-up heart. Plus you've helped my heart grow several sizes.

My three beloved children, Ben, Josh, and Anna (Kenyon), with a major love shout-out to their spouses (respectively, Jerusha, Shayna, and Rich). You three bring more joy into my life than you can imagine, and I love the adults you've turned into. It's so nice to not just love your children, but to respect them and enjoy them too. Thank you for allowing that to happen. *Et Gautier Grellety, tu es inclus ici! Toujours mon fils français!*

Doug Hickerson, Tiffany Dawn (Robison), and Christopher Hopper, who by their example showed me that I too was a writer and that this book could be done.

David Sluka, my editor and encourager. May this book be as much of a blessing to you as you have been to me.

Glenn Baron, who showed me you can act like a grown-up and still be a kid at heart.

Rupert VanHooft, who had even less help than I did with growing up when he was younger. Rupe, you continue to work at the difficult task of growing up when other adults have long given up. You're an inspiration.

About the Author

MARK DUPRÉ is a writer, musician, film professor, and pastor. He is currently teaching at Rochester Institute of Technology, an incredible institution doing amazing work. His main class is called Introduction to Film, which doesn't mean much of anything except to administrators. The class goes into *how* the art of film works, delving into cinematography, color, mise-en-scène, editing, acting, screenplay, and more. It's a totally cool class, and a stress-reliever for the professor, believe it or not.

He blogs about films and provides film reviews at www.film-prof.com. He has the nerve to do this blog because he has two degrees from Columbia University in film, and most people don't. Plus he's really getting up there in age, and the only upside to that is that he has some thinking and history to draw on. Plus he's had enough experience working for various publications that his writing isn't completely embarrassing.

Mark is also an associate pastor of Christ Community Church in Brockport, New York (near Rochester) where he preaches, teaches, counsels, marries/buries, edits the bulletin, strategically plans with the senior pastor, and oversees the worship, music, and arts. He loves truth, beauty, and excellence, probably in that order. He is very opinionated, and can occasionally back that up. He's also intense, or so all his friends say.

On the personal side, he's been married for forty years to his first wife (the beautiful and talented Diane), has three married children, and perhaps the cutest grandchildren ever (though he might be prejudiced there).

Connect with Mark and sign up to receive a daily, inspirational devotional at

www.markdupre.com

Download a discussion guide for this book at

www.actlikeagrownup.com

Endnotes

1 Centers for Disease Control and Prevention. Web-based Injury Statistics Query and Reporting System (WISQARS) [Online]. (2012). National Center for Injury Prevention and Control, Centers for Disease Control and Prevention (producer). [Cited 2014 Sept 29]. See http://www.cdc.gov/motorvehiclesafety/teen_drivers/teendrivers_factsheet.html.

2 Insurance Institute for Highway Safety (IIHS). Fatality facts: teenagers 2012. Arlington (VA): The Institute; 2012 [cited 2014 Sept 29]. http://www.iihs.org/iihs/topics/t/teenagers/fatalityfacts/teenagers.

3 Finkelstein EA, Corso PS, Miller TR, Associates. Incidence and Economic Burden of Injuries in the United States. New York: Oxford University Press; 2006. See http://www.cdc.gov/motorvehiclesafety/teen_drivers/teendrivers_factsheet.html.

4 "Suicide Facts," SAVE (Suicide Awareness Voices of Education). See www.save.org/facts.

5 "Thomas A. Edison quotes," Goodreads.com. See http://www.goodreads.com/author/quotes/3091287.Thomas_A_Edison.

Notes

Notes

Notes

www.actlikeagrownup.com